NATIVE AMERICANA

Native Americana
Author: Kambiz Mostofizadeh
Publisher: Mikazuki Publishing House
ISBN-13: 978-1942825074
Copyright 2016 by Kambiz Mostofizadeh
Desc: Learn the history, wisdom, and knowledge of the Native Americans.
Except for use in a review, the reproduction or utilization of this work in any form or by an electronic, mechanical, or other means, now known or hereafter invented, including xerography, photocopying, recording, in any information storage and retrieval system, is forbidden and prohibited without the written permission of the author.
DISCLAIMER: THE PUBLISHER AND AUTHOR ACCEPT NO RESPONSIBILITY FOR YOUR ACTIONS BASED ON THIS BOOK.
The information contained within this book is for educational and commercial purposes and does not necessarily reflect the views of the publisher.

NATIVE AMERICANA

Kachina Doll

NATIVE AMERICANA

INTRODUCTION

The Native Americans. One of the greatest peoples that have ever lived on this earth. Their bravery is un-matched, their purity is un-rivaled, and their wisdom leaves us all yearning to learn more. Their words and deeds are known well throughout the world. Their love of the environment, their collective hospitality, and their beautiful designs, have inspired countless individuals. Researching in the creation of this book taught me many things about the beautiful culture and customs of the Native American people. I hope you take as much joy in reading it as I did in creating it. Enjoy.

Sincerely,
Kambiz Mostofizadeh, Author

NATIVE AMERICANA

TABLE OF CONTENTS

Origin of Native Americans – 8

Medicine & Medicine Men – 20

Culture and Customs – 26

The Policy - 40

Westward Ho! – 43

Anasazi – 47

Powers of the Tribal Council – 71

Quotes about Native Americans – 80

Wisdom of Native Americans – 91

Native American Weapons – 99

Native American Tribes – 101

Last Word - 127

Notes - 128

NATIVE AMERICANA

Native American male (probably in his mid-30's)

THE NATIVE AMERICAN CREED

(1) One Supreme Spirit

(2) Immortality of the soul

(3) Sacredness of body

(4) Asceticism – Less consumption

(5) Respect for Elders

(6) Property is sacred. Theft is non-existent.

(7) Eye for an Eye

(8) Cleanliness

(9) Purity of morals.

(10) Truth

(11) Beautification of environment

(12) Collectivism and simple life

(13) Hospitality and that visitor is sacred.

(14) Courage

(15) Life without regret

NATIVE AMERICANA

Hiawatha as a small boy

NATIVE AMERICANA

ORIGIN OF NATIVE AMERICANS

At the height of the Ice Age, between 34,000 and 30,000 B.C., much of the world's water was locked up in vast continental ice sheets. As a result, the Bering Sea was hundreds of meters below its current level, and a land bridge, known as Beringia, emerged between Asia and North America. At its peak, Beringia is thought to have been some 1,500 kilometers wide. A moist and treeless tundra, it was covered with grasses and plant life, attracting the large animals that early humans hunted for their survival. The first people to reach North America almost certainly did so without knowing they had crossed into a new continent. They would have been following game, as their ancestors had for thousands of years, along the Siberian coast and then across the land bridge. Once in Alaska, it

NATIVE AMERICANA

Native American hunting

NATIVE AMERICANA

would take these first North Americans thousands of years more to work their way through the openings in great glaciers south to what is now the United States. Evidence of early life in North America continues to be found. Little of it, however, can be reliably dated before 12,000 B.C.; a recent discovery of a hunting lookout in northern Alaska, for example, may date from almost that time. So too may the finely crafted spear points and items found near Clovis, New Mexico.

Similar artifacts have been found at sites throughout North and South America, indicating that life was probably already well established in much of the Western Hemisphere by some time prior to 10,000 B.C. Around that time the mammoth began to die out and the bison took its place as a principal source of food and hides for these early North

Americans. Over time, as more and more species of large game vanished — whether from overhunting or natural causes — plants, berries, and seeds became an increasingly important part of the early American diet. Gradually, foraging and the first attempts at primitive agriculture appeared. Native Americans in what is now central Mexico led

NATIVE AMERICANA

the way, cultivating corn, squash, and beans, perhaps as early as 8,000 B.C. Slowly, this knowledge spread northward. By 3,000 B.C., a primitive type of corn was being grown in the river valleys of New Mexico and Arizona. Then the first signs of irrigation began to appear, and, by 300 B.C., signs of early village life. By the first centuries A.D., the Hohokam were living in settlements near what is now Phoenix, Arizona, where they built ball courts and pyramid-like mounds reminiscent of those found in Mexico, as well as a canal and irrigation system. The first Native-American group to build mounds in what is now the United States often are called the Adenans. They began constructing earthen burial sites and fortifications around 600 B.C. Some mounds from that era are in the shape of birds or serpents; they probably served religious

NATIVE AMERICANA

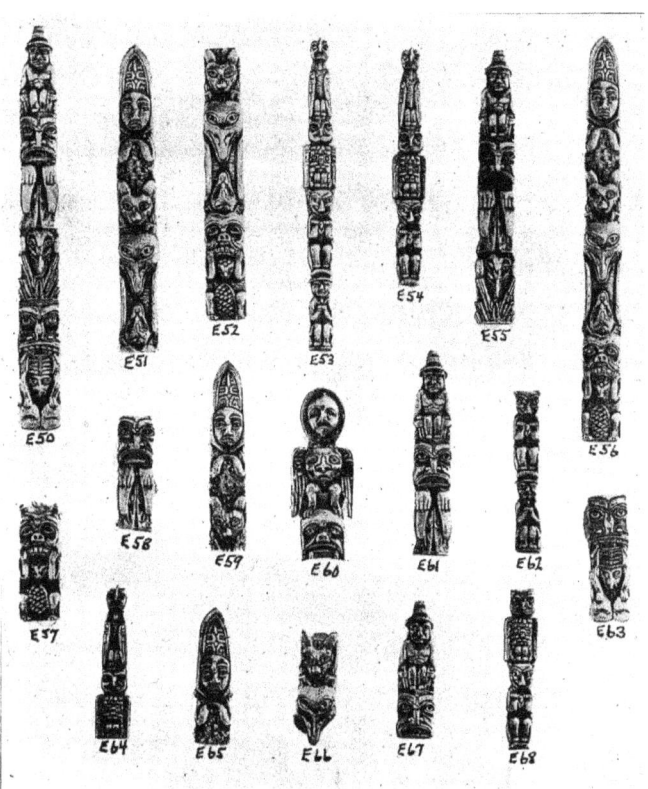

Totems

purposes not yet fully understood. The Adenans appear to have been absorbed or displaced by various groups collectively known as Hopewellians. One of the most important centers of their culture was found in southern Ohio, where the remains of several thousand of these mounds still can be seen. Believed to be great traders, the Hopewellians used and exchanged tools and materials across a wide region of hundreds of kilometers. By around 500 A.D., the Hopewellians disappeared, too, gradually giving way to a broad group of tribes generally known as the Mississippians or Temple Mound culture. One city, Cahokia, near Collinsville, Illinois, is thought to have had a population of about 20,000 at its peak in the early 12th century. At the center of the city stood a huge earthen mound, flattened at the top, that was 30 meters high and 37 hectares

NATIVE AMERICANA

British soldiers accepting an Indian envoy

at the base. Eighty other mounds have been found nearby. Cities such as Cahokia depend-

NATIVE AMERICANA

ed on a combination of hunting, foraging, trading, and agriculture for their food and supplies. Influenced by the thriving societies to the south, they evolved into complex hierarchical societies that took slaves and practiced human sacrifice.

In what is now the southwest United States, the Anasazi, ancestors of the modern Hopi Indians, began building stone and adobe pueblos around the year 900.These unique and amazing apartment-like structures were often built along cliff faces; the most famous, the "cliff palace" of Mesa Verde, Colorado, had more than 200 rooms. Another site, the Pueblo Bonito ruins along New Mexico's Chaco River, once contained more than 800 rooms.

Perhaps the most affluent of the pre-Columbian Native Americans lived in the Pacific Northwest, where the natural

NATIVE AMERICANA

abundance of fish and raw materials made food supplies plentiful and permanent villages possible as early as 1,000 B.C. The opulence of their "potlatch" gatherings remains a

standard for extravagance and festivity probably unmatched in early American history. The America that greeted the first Europeans was, thus, far from an empty wilderness. It is now thought that as many people lived in the Western Hemisphere as in Western Europe at that time — about 40 million. Estimates of the number of Native Americans living in what is now the United States at the onset of European colonization range from two to 18 million, with most historians tending toward the lower figure. What is certain is the devastating effect that European disease had on the indigenous population practically from the time of initial contact. Smallpox, in particular, ravaged whole communities and is thought to have been a much more direct cause of the precipitous decline in the Indian population in

NATIVE AMERICANA

the 1600s than the numerous wars and skirmishes with European settlers.

Native American Medicine Man

MEDICINE AND MEDICINE MEN

Medicine is an agent or influence employed to prevent, alleviate, or cure some pathological condition or its symptoms. The scope of such agents among the Indians was extensive, ranging, as among other primitive peoples, from magic, prayer, force of suggestion, and a multitude of symbolic and empirical means, to actual and more rationally used remedies. Where the Indians are in contact with whites the old methods of combating physical ills are slowly giving way to the curative agencies of civilization. The white man in turn has adopted from the Indians a number of valuable medicinal plants, such as cinchona, jalapa, hydrastis, etc. In general the tribes show many similarities in regard to medicine, but the actual agents employed differ with the tribes and localities, as well as with individual healers. Magic, prayers, songs, exhortation, suggestion, ceremonies, fetishes, and certain specifics and mechanical processes are employed only by the medicine-men or medicine-women; other specific remedies or procedures are proprietary, generally among a few old women in the tribe; while many vegetal remedies and simple manipulations are of common knowledge in a given locality. The employment of magic consists in opposing a supposed malign influence, such as that of a sorcerer, spirits of the dead, mythic animals, etc., by the super-natural power of the healer's fetishes and other means. Prayers are addressed to benevolent deities and spirits, invoking their aid. Healing songs, consisting of prayers or exhortations, are sung. Harangues are directed to evil spirits supposed to cause the sickness, and often are accentuated by noises to frighten such spirits away. Suggestion is exercised in many ways directly and indirectly. Curative ceremonies usually combine all or most of the agencies mentioned. Some of them, such as Matthews describes among the Navaho, are very elaborate, prolonged, and costly. The fetishes used are peculiarly shaped stones or wooden objects, lightning-hit wood, feathers, claws, hair, figurines of mythic animals, representations of the sun, of lightning, etc., and are supposed to embody a mysterious power capable of preventing disease or of counteracting its effects. The ordinary procedure of the medicine-man was about as follows: He inquired into the symptoms, dreams, and transgressions of tabus of the patient, whom he examined, and then pronounced his opinion as to the nature (generally mythical) of the ailment. He then prayed, exhorted, or sang, the last, perhaps, to the accompaniment of a rattle; made passes with his hand, sometimes moistened with saliva, over the part affected; and finally placed his mouth over the most painful spot and sucked hard to extract the immediate principle of the illness. This result he apparently accomplished, often by means of sleight-of-hand, producing the offending cause in the shape of a thorn, pebble, hair, or other object, which was then thrown away or destroyed; finally he administered a mysterious powder or other tangible "medicine," and perhaps left also a protective fetish. There were many variations of this method, according to the requirements of the case, and the medicine-man never failed to exercise as much mental influence as possible over his patient. For these services the healer was usually well compensated. If the case would not yield to the simpler treatment, a healing ceremony might be resorted to. If all means failed, particularly in the case of internal diseases or of adolescents or younger adults, the medicine-man often suggested a witch or wizard as the cause, and the designation of someone as the culprit frequently placed his life in jeopardy. If the medicine-man lost several patients in succession, he himself might be suspected either of having been deprived of his supernatural power or of having become a sorcerer, the penalty for which was usually death. These shaman healers as a rule were shrewd and experienced men; some were sincere, noble characters, worthy of respect; others were charlatans to a greater or less degree. They are still to be found among the less civilized tribes, but are diminishing in number and losing their influence. Medicine-women of this class were found among the Apache and some other tribes.

The most accomplished of the medicine-men practiced also a primitive surgery, and aided, by external manipulation and otherwise, in difficult labor. The highest surgical achievement, undoubtedly practiced in part at least as a curative method, was trephining. This operation was of common occurrence and is still practiced in Peru, where it reached its highest development among American tribes.

CULTURE AND CUSTOMS

Indian customs and culture at the time were extraordinarily diverse, as could be expected, given the expanse of the land and the many different environments to which they had adapted. Some generalizations, however, are possible. Most tribes, particularly in the wooded eastern region and the Midwest, combined aspects of hunting, gathering, and the cultivation of maize and other products for their food supplies.

If we are indebted to the Indians for maize, "without which the peopling of America would probably have been delayed for a century, it is also from them that the whites learned the methods of planting, storing, and using it."
-Hodge

In many cases, the women were responsible for farming and the distribution of food, while the men hunted and participated in war.

NATIVE AMERICANA

By all accounts, Native-American society in North America was closely tied to the land.

NATIVE AMERICANA

Identification with nature and the elements was integral to religious beliefs. Their life was essentially clan-oriented and communal, with children allowed more freedom and tolerance than was the European custom of the day. Although some North American tribes developed a type of hieroglyphics to preserve certain texts, Native-American culture was primarily oral, with a high value placed on the recounting of tales and dreams. Clearly, there was a good deal of trade among various groups and strong evidence exists that neighboring tribes maintained extensive and formal relations — both friendly and hostile. Land was viewed as communal property and if it was sold, the proceeds were split between members of the tribe. For example, in 1624, the island was purchased from local Native Americans for the reported price of $24.

NATIVE AMERICANA

Collectivism played a major role in the affairs of the tribe and all members were viewed as responsible for each other. By 1640 the British had solid colonies established along the New England coast and the Chesapeake Bay. In between were the Dutch and the tiny Swedish community. To the west were the original Native Americans, then called Indians. Sometimes friendly, sometimes hostile, the

Native American Tribal Banner made of Bow & Arrows

Eastern tribes were no longer strangers to the Europeans. Although Native Americans benefited from access to new technology and trade, the disease and thirst for land that the early settlers also brought posed a serious challenge to their long-established way of life. At first, trade with the European settlers brought advantages: knives, axes, weapons, cooking utensils, fishhooks, and a host of other goods. Those Indians who traded initially had significant advantage over rivals who did not. In response to European demand, tribes such as the Iroquois began to devote more attention to fur trapping during the 17th century. Furs and pelts provided tribes the means to purchase colonial goods until late into the 18th century. Early colonial-Native-American relations were an uneasy mix of cooperation and conflict. On the one hand, there were the exemplary relations that prevailed during the first half century of Pennsylvania's existence. On the other were a long series of setbacks, skirmishes, and wars, which almost invariably resulted in an Indian defeat and further loss of

NATIVE AMERICANA

land. The first of the important Native-American uprisings occurred in Virginia in 1622, when some 347 whites were killed, including a number of missionaries who had just recently come to Jamestown.

White settlement of the Connecticut River region touched off the Pequot War in 1637. In 1675 King Philip, the son of the native chief who had made the original peace with the Pilgrims in 1621, attempted to unite the tribes of southern New England against further European encroachment of their lands. In the struggle, however, Philip lost his life and many Indians were sold into servitude.

The steady influx of settlers into the backwoods regions of the Eastern colonies disrupted Native-American life. As more and more game was killed off, tribes were faced with the difficult choice of going hungry, going to war, or moving and coming into conflict with other tribes to the west. The Iroquois, who

William Penn seeking peace treaty with Native Americans

inhabited the area below lakes Ontario and Erie in northern New York and Pennsylvania, were more successful in resisting European advances. In 1570 five tribes joined to form the most complex Native-American nation of its time, the "Ho-De-No-Sau-Nee," or League of

the Iroquois. The league was run by a council made up of 50 representatives from each of the five member tribes. The council dealt with matters common to all the tribes, but it had no say in how the free and equal tribes ran their day to-day affairs. No tribe was allowed to make war by itself. The council passed laws to deal with crimes such as murder. The Iroquois League was a strong power in the 1600s and 1700s. It traded furs with the British and sided with them against the French in the war for the dominance of America between 1754 and 1763. The British might not have won that war otherwise. The Iroquois League stayed strong until the American Revolution.
Then, for the first time, the council could not reach a unanimous decision on whom to support. Member tribes made their own decisions, some fighting with the British,

Native American Spiritual Shield

some with the colonists, some remaining neutral. As a result, everyone fought against the Iroquois. Their losses were great and the league never recovered. In the Greenville treaty of 1795, between the United States and representatives of the Hurons, Delawares,

NATIVE AMERICANA

Ottawa, Chippewa, Potawatomi, Sauk, and other tribes, a part of the function, involved the presentation of peace medals. The medal in this case was a facsimile of the oval Red Jacket medal, in silver, engraved and chased, with a change in the date to 1795. During the second administration of President George Washington, in 1796, there was issued a series of four Peace Medals, in silver and bronze, called the Season medals. The steady westward pressure of the colonists, together with their policy of fomenting intertribal wars, caused the continual displacement of many native communities, a condition that bore heavily on the semi sedentary tribes, like the Arikara, who lived in villages and cultivated the soil. Almost continuous warfare with aggressive tribes, together with the ravages of smallpox during the latter half of the 18th and the beginning of the 19th centuries, nearly exterminated some of their villages. The weakened survivors consolidated to form new, necessarily composite villages, so that much of their ancient organization was greatly modified or ceased to exist. It was during this period of stress that the Arikara became close neighbors and, finally, allies of the Mandan and Hidatsa. The Arikara were a loosely organized confederacy of subtribes, each of which had its separate village and distinctive name. Few of these names have been preserved. Lewis and Clark mention Lahoocat, a village occupied in 1797, but abandoned about 1800. How many subtribes were included in the confederacy cannot now be determined. Lewis and Clark speak of the Arikara as the remnant of 10 powerful

NATIVE AMERICANA

Pawnee tribes, living in 1804 in 3 villages. The inroads of disease and war have so reduced the tribe that little now remains of their former divisions. In 1804, when Lewis and Clark visited the Arikara, they were disposed to be friendly to the United States, but, owing to intrigues incident to the rivalry between trading companies, which brought suffering to the Indians, they became hostile. In the sign language the Arikara are designated as "corn eaters," the movement of the hand simulating the act of gnawing the kernels of corn from the cob. They preserved the seed of a peculiar kind of small-eared corn, said to be very nutritious and much liked. It is also said that the seed corn was kept tied in a skin and hung up in the lodge near the fireplace, and when the time for planting came only those kernels showing signs of germination were

NATIVE AMERICANA

used. The Arikara bartered corn with the Cheyenne and other tribes for buffalo robes, skins, and meat, and exchanged these with the traders for cloth, cooking utensils, guns, etc. Early dealings with the traders were carried on by the women. The Arikara hunted the buffalo in winter, returning to their village in the early spring, where they spent the time before planting in dressing the pelts. Their fish supply was obtained by means of basket traps. They were expert swimmers, and ventured to capture buffaloes that were disabled in the water as the herd was crossing the river. Their wood supply was obtained from the river; when the ice broke up in the spring the Indians leaped on the cakes, attached cords to the trees that were whirling down the rapid current, and hauled them ashore. Men, women, and the older children engaged in this exciting work, and although they sometimes fell and were swept downstream, their dexterity and courage generally prevented serious accident. Their boats were made of a single buffalo skin stretched, hair side in, over a frame of willows bent round like a basket and tied to a hoop 3 or 4 feet in diameter.

NATIVE AMERICANA

THE POLICY

It was the usual policy of the United States and other governments, as well as of the colonies, in dealing with the Indians to treat them as tribes. The Articles of Confederation gave to Congress the "sole and exclusive right and power of regulating the trade and managing all affairs with the Indians" not under State jurisdiction. By the Constitution, the power of Congress in this respect is briefly expressed as follows: "To regulate commerce with foreign nations and among the several States, and with the Indian tribes." The authority to act in this respect must therefore be found in this clause, in that relating to the making of treaties, and in the general powers granted to Congress and the Executive. The term "tribes" in the clause quoted would indicate that the framers of the Constitution contemplated dealing with

NATIVE AMERICANA

the Indians as autonomous groups, through treaties; this was the method followed by the United States until it was changed by the act of Mar. 3, 1871, and was that of the colonies and the mother country. The effect of the act cited was to bring under the immediate control of Congress, as specified in art. i, section 8, clause 3, of the Constitution, all transactions with the Indians, and to reduce to simple agreements what before had been accomplished by solemn treaties. Laws were enacted in the various colonies, and also by the United States, forbidding and rendering void the sale of lands by Indians to individuals. By the act of Congress of Feb. 8, 1887, the later policy of the Government, that the Indian tribes should cease to exist as independent communities and be made part of the body politic, found legislative expression. This act permits tribal lands, including reservations, to be divided so as to give to each man, woman, and child of the tribe an individual holding and, after a limited probation, confers citizenship upon the allottees, and makes them subject to the laws of the states or territories within which they live. Previous, however, to this final step intervened the reservation policy. The plan of forming Indian reservations was adopted from the necessity of bringing tribes under the more complete control of the Government and of confining them to definite limits for the better preservation of order, and aimed especially to restrict them to less territory in order that the whites might obtain the use of the residue. This was a most important step in the process of leading the natives to abandon the hunter stage and to depend for their subsistence on agriculture and home industries (see Reservations). The same policy was followed in Canada under both French and English rule, and to some extent by the colonies, and it was inaugurated by the United States in 1786.

WESTWARD HO!
Westward expansion brought settlers into conflict with the original inhabitants of the land: the Native Americans. In the first part of the 19th century, the most prominent figure associated with these conflicts was Andrew Jackson, the first "Westerner" to occupy the White House. In the midst of the War of 1812, Jackson, then in charge of the Tennessee militia, was sent into southern Alabama, where he ruthlessly put down an uprising of Creek Indians. The Creeks soon ceded two-thirds of

their land to the United States. Jackson later routed bands of Seminoles from their sanctuaries in Spanish-owned Florida.
In the 1820s, President Monroe's secretary of war, John Calhoun, pursued a policy of removing the remaining tribes from the old Southwest and resettling them beyond the

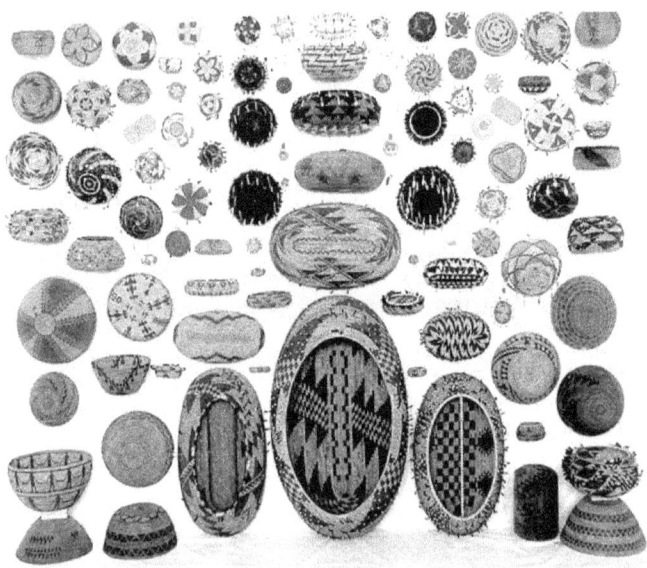

Native American Baskets

NATIVE AMERICANA

Mississippi. Jackson continued this policy as President. In 1830 Congress passed the Indian Removal Act, providing funds to transport the eastern tribes beyond the Mississippi. The Indian Removal Act was the beginning of the end for the various Native American tribes inhabiting North America. In 1834 a special Native American territory was set up in what is now Oklahoma. In all, the tribes signed 94 treaties during Jackson's two terms, ceding millions of hectares to the federal government and removing dozens of tribes from their ancestral homelands. The most terrible chapter in this unhappy history concerned the Cherokees, whose lands in
western North Carolina and Georgia had been guaranteed by treaty since 1791.Among the most progressive of the eastern tribes, the Cherokees nevertheless were sure to be dis-

NATIVE AMERICANA

placed when gold was discovered on their land in 1829. Forced to make a long and cruel trek to Oklahoma in 1838, the tribe lost many of its numbers from disease and privation on what became known as the "Trail of Tears."

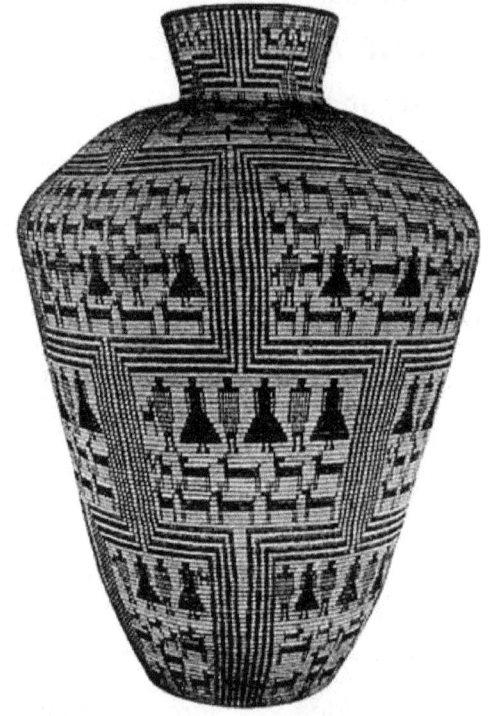

Native American hand woven Basket

NATIVE AMERICANA

ANASAZI

Time-worn pueblos and dramatic cliff towns, set amid the stark, rugged mesas and canyons of Colorado and New Mexico, mark the settlements of some of the earliest inhabitants of North America, the Anasazi (a Navajo word meaning "ancient ones"). By 500 A.D. the Anasazi had established some of the first villages in the American Southwest, where they hunted and grew crops of corn, squash, and beans. The Anasazi flourished over the centuries, developing sophisticated dams and irrigation systems; creating a masterful, distinctive pottery tradition; and carving multi-room dwellings into the sheer sides of cliffs that remain among the most striking archaeological sites in the United States today. Yet by the year 1300, they had abandoned their settlements, leaving their pottery, implements,

NATIVE AMERICANA

Native American Music in Sheet Music form

NATIVE AMERICANA

even clothing as though they intended to return and seemingly vanished into history. Their homeland remained empty of human beings for more than a century until the arrival of new tribes, such as the Navajo and the Ute, followed by the Spanish and other European settlers.

The story of the Anasazi is tied inextricably to the beautiful but harsh environment in which they chose to live. Early settlements, consisting of simple pit houses scooped out of the ground, evolved into sunken kivas (underground rooms) that served as meeting and religious sites. Later generations developed the masonry techniques for building square, stone pueblos. But the most dramatic change in Anasazi living was the move to the cliff sides below the flat-topped mesas, where the Anasazi carved their amazing, multilevel

NATIVE AMERICANA

Navajo Man

dwellings. The Anasazi lived in a communal society. They traded with other peoples in the region, but signs of warfare are few and

NATIVE AMERICANA

isolated. And although the Anasazi certainly had religious and other leaders, as well as skilled artisans, social or class distinctions were virtually nonexistent.

Religious and social motives undoubtedly played a part in the building of the cliff communities and their final abandonment. But the struggle to raise food in an increasingly difficult environment was probably the paramount factor. As populations grew, farmers planted larger areas on the mesas, causing some communities to farm marginal lands, while others left the mesa tops for the cliffs. But the Anasazi couldn't halt the steady loss of the land's fertility from constant use, nor withstand the region's cyclical droughts. Analysis of tree rings, for example, shows that a drought lasting 23 years, from 1276 to 1299, finally forced the last groups of Anasazi to

NATIVE AMERICANA

leave permanently. Although the Anasazi dispersed from their ancestral homeland, their legacy remains in the remarkable archaeological record that they left behind, and in the Hopi, Zuni, and other Pueblo peoples who are their descendants.

As in the East, expansion into the plains and mountains by miners, ranchers, and settlers led to increasing conflicts with the Native Americans of the West. Many tribes of Native Americans, from the Utes of the Great Basin to the Nez Perces of Idaho, fought the whites at one time or another. But the Sioux of the Northern Plains and the Apache of the Southwest provided the most significant opposition to frontier advance. Led by such resourceful leaders as Red Cloud and Crazy Horse, the Sioux were particularly skilled at

NATIVE AMERICANA

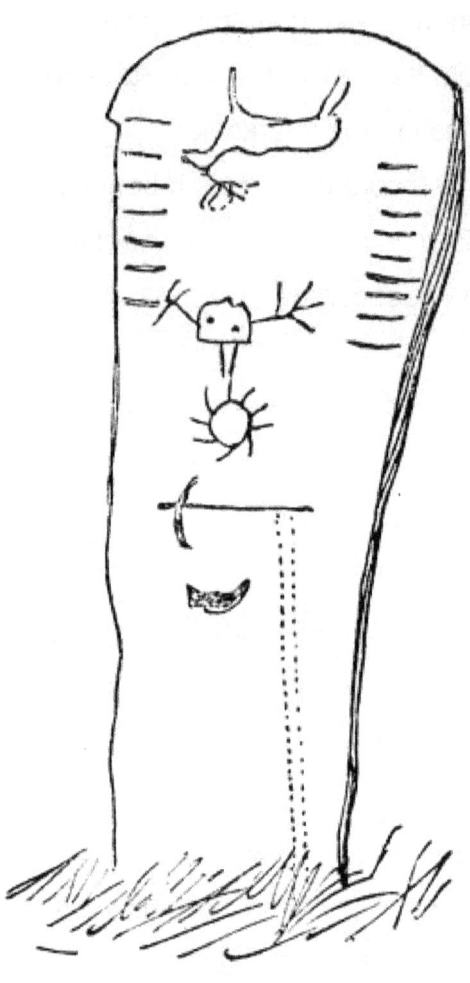

high-speed mounted warfare. The Apaches were equally adept and highly elusive, fighting in their environs of desert and canyons. Conflicts with the Plains Indians worsened after an incident where the Dakota (part of the Sioux nation), declaring war against the U.S.government because of long-standing grievances, killed five white settlers. Rebellions and attacks continued through the Civil War. In 1876 the last serious Sioux war erupted, when the Dakota gold rush penetrated the Black Hills. The Army was supposed to keep miners off Sioux hunting grounds, but did little to protect the Sioux lands. When ordered to take action against bands of Sioux hunting on the range according to their treaty rights, however, it moved quickly and vigorously. In 1876, after several indecisive encounters, Colonel George Custer, leading a small detachment of cavalry

NATIVE AMERICANA

encountered a vastly superior force of Sioux and their allies on the Little Bighorn River. Custer and his men were completely annihilated. Nonetheless the Native-American insurgency was soon suppressed. Later, in 1890, a ghost dance ritual on the Northern Sioux reservation at Wounded Knee, South Dakota, led to an uprising and a last, tragic encounter that ended in the death of nearly 300 Sioux men, women, and children.

Long before this, however, the way of life of the Plains Indians had been destroyed by an expanding white population, the coming of the railroads, and the slaughter of the buffalo, almost exterminated in the decade after 1870 by the settlers' indiscriminate hunting.

The Apache wars in the Southwest dragged on until Geronimo, the last important chief, was captured in 1886. Government policy ever

NATIVE AMERICANA

since the Monroe administration had been to move the Native Americans beyond the reach of the white frontier. But inevitably the

Native American wall drawings

reservations had become smaller and more crowded. Some Americans began to protest the government's treatment of Native Americans. Helen Hunt Jackson, for example, an Easterner living in the West, wrote A Century of Dishonor (1881), which dramatized their plight and struck a chord in the nation's conscience.

Hopi Kachina Helmet

NATIVE AMERICANA

Most reformers believed the Native American should be assimilated into the dominant culture. The federal government even set up a school in Carlisle, Pennsylvania, in an attempt to impose white values and beliefs on Native-American youths.(It was at this school that Jim Thorpe, often considered the best athlete the United States has produced, gained fame in the early 20th century.) In 1887 the Dawes (General Allotment) Act reversed U.S. Native-American policy, permitting the President to divide up

Native American pocket pipe

tribal land and parcel out 65 hectares of land to each head of a family. Such allotments were to be held in trust by the government for 25 years, after which time the owner won full title and citizenship. Lands not thus distributed, however, were offered for sale to settlers. This policy, however well-intentioned, proved disastrous, since it allowed more plundering of Native-American lands. Moreover, its assault on the communal organization of tribes caused further disruption of traditional culture. In 1934 U.S.policy was reversed yet again by the Indian Reorganization Act, which attempted to protect tribal and communal life on the reservations.

In the 1950s, Native Americans struggled with the government's policy of moving them off reservations and into cities where they might

NATIVE AMERICANA

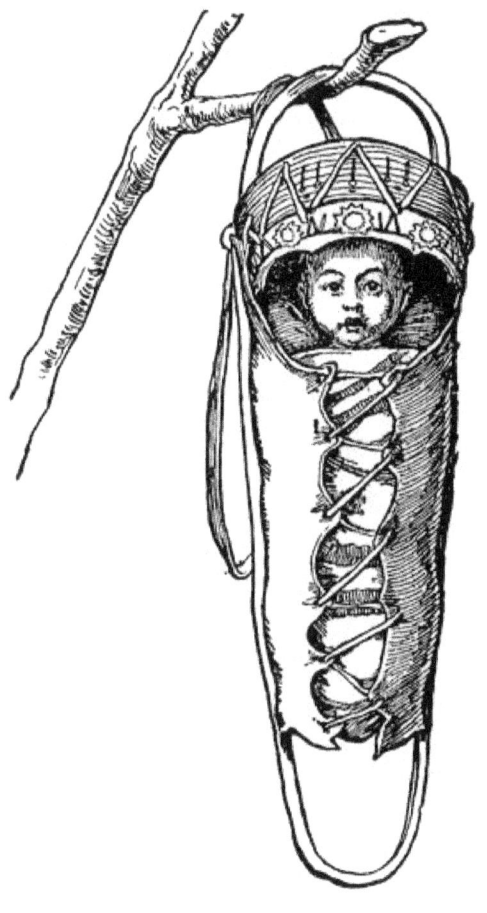

Baby Hiawatha

NATIVE AMERICANA

assimilate into mainstream America. Many of the uprooted often had difficulties adjusting to urban life. In 1961, when the policy was discontinued, the U.S. Commission on Civil Rights noted that, for Native Americans, "poverty and deprivation are common."

In the 1960s and 1970s, watching both the development of Third World nationalism and the progress of the civil rights movement, Native Americans became more aggressive in pressing for their own rights. A new generation of leaders went to court to protect what was left of tribal lands or to recover those which had been taken, often illegally, in previous times. In state after state, they challenged treaty violations, and in 1967 won the first of many victories guaranteeing long-abused land and water rights. The American Indian Movement (AIM), founded in 1968, helped channel

NATIVE AMERICANA

government funds to Native-American-controlled organizations and assisted neglected Native Americans in the cities. Confrontations became more common. In 1969 a landing party of 78 Native Americans seized Alcatraz Island in San Francisco Bay and held it until federal officials removed them in 1971. In 1973 AIM took over the South Dakota village of Wounded Knee, where soldiers in the late 19th century had massacred a Sioux encampment. Militants hoped to dramatize the poverty and alcoholism in the reservation surrounding the town. The episode ended after one Native American was killed and another wounded,

NATIVE AMERICANA

with a government agreement to re-examine treaty rights. Still, Native-American activism brought results. Other Americans became more aware of Native-American needs. Government officials responded with measures including the Education Assistance Act of 1975 and the 1996 Native-American Housing and Self- Determination Act. The Senate's first Native-American member, Ben Nighthorse

NATIVE AMERICANA

Campbell of Colorado, was elected in 1992.

Native Americans wearing masks in ceremony.

NATIVE AMERICANA

RULES OF THE TEEPEE
- Be hospitable.
- Always assume that your guest is tired, cold, and hungry.
- Always give your guest the place of honor in the lodge and at the feast, and serve him in reasonable ways.
- Never sit while your guest stands.
- Go hungry rather than stint your guest.
- If your guest refuses certain food, say nothing; he may be under vow.
- Protect your guest as one of the family; feed his horse, and beat your dogs if they harm his dog.
- Do not trouble your guest with many questions about himself; he will tell you what he wishes you to know.
- In another man's lodge follow his customs, not your own.

NATIVE AMERICANA

- Never worry your host with your troubles.
- Always repay calls of courtesy.
- Give your host a little present on leaving; little presents are little courtesies and never give offence.
- Say "Thank you" for every gift, however small.
- Compliment your host, even if you strain the facts to do so.
- Never walk between persons talking.
- Never interrupt persons talking.
- Let not the young speak among those much older, unless asked.
- Always give place to your seniors in entering or leaving the lodge; or anywhere.
- Never sit while your seniors stand.

NATIVE AMERICANA

- Never force your conversation on any one.
- Speak softly, especially before your elders, or in presence of strangers.
- Never come between anyone & the fire.
- Do not touch live coals with a steel knife or any sharp steel.
- Do not stare at strangers; drop your eyes if they stare hard at you.
- The women of the lodge are the keepers of the fire, but the men should help with the heavier sticks.
- Always give a word or sign of salute when meeting or passing a friend, or even a stranger, if in a lonely place.
- Do not talk to your mother-in-law at any time, or let her talk to you.
- Be kind.

NATIVE AMERICANA

- Show respect to all men, but grovel to none.
- Let silence be your motto till duty bids you

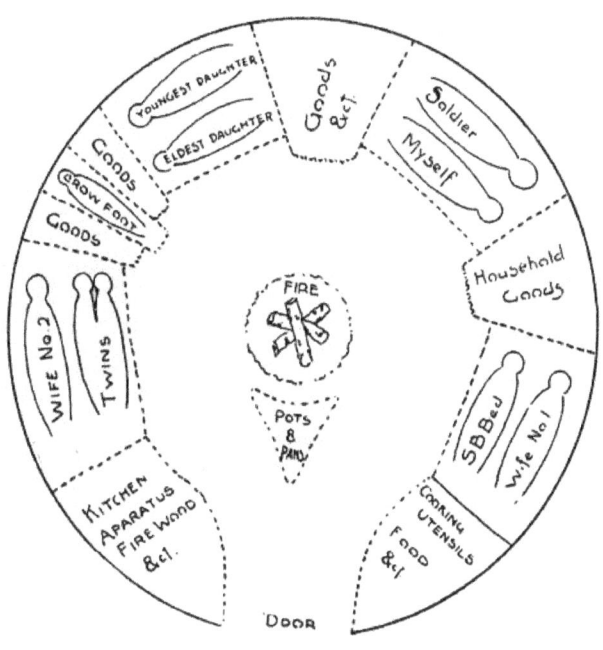

Teepee seating arrangement

NATIVE AMERICANA

Tribal Council

NATIVE AMERICANA

POWERS OF THE TRIBAL COUNCIL

The Tribal Council shall have all powers vested in the Tribe through its inherent sovereignty or federal law. It shall execute these powers in accordance with established customs of the Tribe and subject to the express limitations contained in this constitution or other applicable laws. These powers include but are not limited to the following:

(a) To represent the Tribe and act in all matters that concern the welfare of the Tribe, and to make decisions not inconsistent with or contrary to this constitution;

(b) To negotiate and enter into contracts with the federal, state, local and tribal governments, and with individuals, associations, corporations, enterprises or organizations;

NATIVE AMERICANA

(c) To purchase or accept any land or property for the Tribe;

(d) To enact laws regulating the use, disposition and inheritance of all property within the territory of the Tribe;

(e) To prevent or veto the sale, disposition, lease or encumbrance of tribal lands, interests in land, tribal funds or other tribal assets;

(f) To employ legal counsel in accordance with applicable federal laws;

(g) To enact laws regulating the domestic relations of persons within the jurisdiction of the Tribe;

NATIVE AMERICANA

(h) To enact a law and order code governing the conduct of persons within the jurisdiction of the Tribe in accordance with applicable laws;

(i) To provide for the removal or exclusion of any non-member of the Tribe whose presence maybe injurious to members of the Tribe, and to prescribe conditions upon which non-members may remain within the territory of the Tribe;

(j) To levy and collect taxes, duties, fees and assessments;

(k) To appropriate and regulate the use of tribal funds in accordance with an annual budget approved by the Tribal Council;

(l) To regulate all business activities within the jurisdiction of the Tribe, and to manage all tribal economic affairs and enterprises;

(m) To regulate all matters and to take all actions necessary to preserve and safeguard the health, safety, welfare and political integrity of the Tribe;

(n) To appoint subordinate committees, commissions, boards, tribal officers and employees, and to set their compensation, tenure and duties;

(o) To enact laws, ordinances and resolutions necessary or incidental to the exercise of its legislative powers;

(p) To take any and all actions necessary and proper for the exercise of the foregoing powers and duties, including those powers and duties not enumerated above, and for all other powers and duties now or hereafter delegated to the Tribal Council, or vested in the Tribe by federal law or through its inherent sovereignty.

Hopi Indians; Three Snake Priests

NATIVE AMERICANA

Native American Tribal Chief with Peace Pipe

NATIVE AMERICANA

NATIVE AMERICAN POLITICAL VALUES

- Promote the common good and well-being of the Tribe;
- Protect and preserve culture and traditions including language, arts and crafts, and archeological sites;
- Protect land, water and natural resources;
- Promote and protect the health and welfare of Native American people;
- Encourage and promote educational opportunities for members of the Tribe;
- Foster economic development;
- Protect the individual rights of tribal members;
- Acquire additional lands for the benefit of the Tribe;
- Promote self-government and ensure the political integrity of the Tribe;

NATIVE AMERICANA

- Preserve, secure and exercise all the inherent sovereign rights and powers of an Indian tribe.

NATIVE AMERICANA

QUOTES ABOUT NATIVE AMERICANS

"The Cheyenne women are retiring and modest, and for chastity will compare favorably with women of any other nation or people, almost models of purity and chastity."
- Colonel Dodge

"Their women are beautiful and modest and amongst the respectable families, virtue is as highly cherished and as inapproachable, as in any society whatever."
- George Caitlin

"Adultery is esteemed by them a heinous crime, and punished with the greatest rigor."
- Jonathan Carver

"The greatest insult that can be offered to an Indian, is, to doubt his courage."

NATIVE AMERICANA

- JD Hunter

"They are high-minded and proud; possess a courage equal to every trial; an intrepid valor; the most heroic constancy under torments, and an equanimity which neither misfortune nor reverses can shake."
- Father Lafitau

"I have never known a solitary instance of their wantonly destroying any of those animals [buffalo, elk, and deer], except on the hunting-grounds of their enemies, or encouraged to it by the prospect of bartering their skins with the traders."
- JD Hunter

"There is scarcely anything so exasperating to me as the idea that the natives of this country

NATIVE AMERICANA

have no sense of humor and no faculty for mirth. This phase of their character is well understood by those whose fortune or misfortune it has been to live among then, day in and day out, at their homes. I don't believe I ever heard a real hearty laugh away from the Indians' fireside. I have often spent an entire evening in laughter with them, until I could laugh no more. There are evenings when the recognized wit or story-teller of the village gives a free entertainment which keeps the rest of the community in a convulsive state until he leaves them. However, Indian humor consists as much in the gestures and inflections of the voice, as in words, and is really untranslatable."
- Eastman

NATIVE AMERICANA

"The common belief that the Indian is stoical, stolid, and sullen, is all together erroneous. They are really a merry people, good-natured and jocular, usually ready to laugh at an amusing incident or a joke, with a simple mirth that reminds one of children."
- Grinnell

NATIVE AMERICANA

"I have seen white men reduced to the last 'hard tack,' with only tobacco enough for two smokes, and with no immediate prospect of anything better than horse-meat 'straight.' A portion of the hard bread was hidden away, and the smokes were taken in secret. An Indian, un-demoralized by contact with the whites, under similar circumstances, would divide down to the last morsel."
- Clark

NATIVE AMERICANA

"The most shameful chapter of American history is that in which is recorded the account of our dealings with the Indians. The story of our Government's intercourse with this race is an unbroken narrative of injustice, fraud and robbery."
- John G. Bourke

"Two men from a trading expedition in the Indian country called on me to-day. They state that one half of the furs purchased in the Indian country are obtained in exchange for whiskey. They also stated that the Cheyennes, a tribe of Indians on the Platte River, were wholly averse to drinking whiskey, but, five years ago — now (through the influence of a trader, Captain Gant, who, by sweetening the whiskey, induced them to drink the intoxicating draught), they are a tribe of drunkards."

NATIVE AMERICANA

- Moses Merrill

"They were friendly in their dispositions, honest to the most scrupulous degree in their intercourse with the white man. Simply to call these people religious would convey but a faint idea of the deep hue of piety and devotion which pervades their whole conduct. Their honesty is immaculate, and their purity of purpose and their observance of the rites of their religion are most uniform and remarkable. They are certainly more like a nation of saints than a horde of savages."
- Washington Irving

"History can show no parallel to the heroism and fortitude of the American Indians in the two hundred years' fight during which they contested inch by inch the possession of their country against a foe infinitely better equipped, with inexhaustible resources, and in overwhelming numbers. Had they even been equal in numbers, history might have had a very different story to tell. "

- Unknown Indian Fighter

NATIVE AMERICANA

"I am afraid we have stamped out a system that was producing men who, taken all around, were better than ourselves."
- Professor Nichols

"The Tarahumare mail carrier from Chihuahua to Batopilas, Mexico, runs regularly more than 500 miles a week; a Hopi messenger has been known to run 120 miles in 15 hours."
- Hodge

"In legislation, in eloquence, in fortitude, and in military sagacity, they had no equals. Crimes and offences were so infrequent, under their social system, that the Iroquois can scarcely be said to have had a criminal code."
- Morgan

NATIVE AMERICANA

"We shall find them temperate, both in their diet and potations that they withstand with unexampled patience, the attacks of hunger, or the inclemency of the seasons, and esteem the gratification of their appetites but as a secondary consideration."

- Morgan

"The three principal causes of wars with the Indians are first, non-fulfilment of treaties by the United States Government. Second, fraud by the Indian agents. Third, encroachments by the whites."

- Colonel Dodge

"On all occasions, and at whatever price, the Iroquois spoke the truth, without fear and without hesitation."

- Morgan

NATIVE AMERICANA

"Politeness is shown by men to women. Men used to help women and children to alight from horses. When they had to ford streams, the men used to assist them, and sometimes they carried them across on their backs."
- Professor Dorsey

"Among the Iroquoian tribe, the Susquehanna, the Hurons, and the Iroquois, the penalties for killing a woman of the tribe were double those exacted for the killing of a man, because in the death of a woman, the Iroquoian lawgivers recognized the probable loss of a long line of prospective offspring."
- Hodge

"Bad as the savages are, they never violate the chastity of any woman, their prisoners."
- Colonel Van Schaick

NATIVE AMERICANA

THE WISDOM OF TSHUT-CHE-NAU, CHIEF OF THE KANSAS

- When you become men be brave and cunning in war, and defend your hunting grounds against all encroachments.

- Never suffer your squaws or little ones to want.

- Protect the squaws and strangers from insult.

- On no account betray your friend.

- Resent insults.

- Revenge yourself on your enemies.

- Drink not the poisonous strong water of the white people; it is sent by the Bad Spirit to destroy the Indians.

- Fear not death; none but cowards fear to die.

THE WISDOM OF SKUR-AR-ALE-SHAR, LONE CHIEF

- When you get to be a man remember that it is ambition that makes the man.

- If you go on the warpath do not turn around when you have gone part way, but go on as far as you were going; then come back.

NATIVE AMERICANA

- If I should live to see you become a man I want you to become a great man. I want you to think about the hard times we have been through.

- Take pity on people who are poor, because we have been poor, and people have taken pity on us.

- If I live to see you a man, and to go off on the warpath, I would not cry if I were to hear that you had been killed in battle. That is what makes a man, to fight and to be brave.

- Love your friend and never desert him. If you see him surrounded by the enemy do not run away; go to him, and if you cannot save him, be lulled together, and let your bones lie side by side.

WISDOM OF WABASHA

- In the day of his strength no man is fat. Fat is good in a beast, but in a man it is disease and comes only of an evil life. No man will eat three times each sun if he would keep his body strong and his mind unclouded.

- Bathe every sun in cold water and one sun in seven enters the sweat lodge.

- If you would purify your heart and so see clearer the way of the Great Spirit, touch no food for two days or more, according to your strength. For thereby your spirit hath mastery over the body and the body is purged.

- Touch not the poisonous firewater that makes wise men turn fools. Neither touch food nor taste drink that robs the body of its power or the spirit.

- Guard your tongue in youth, and in age you may mature a thought that will be of service to your people.

- Praise God when you rise, when you bathe, when you eat, when you meet your friends and for all good happenings.

NATIVE AMERICANA

- And if so be you see no cause for praise the fault is in yourself.

- You should be at all times clean, courteous and master of yourself.

- The wise man will not hurt his mind for the passing pleasure of the body.

- If any man be given over to sex appetite he is harboring a rattlesnake, whose sting is rottenness and sure death.

- By prayer and fasting and fixed purpose you can rule your own spirit, and so have power over all those about you.

- When your time comes to die, sing your death song and die pleasantly, not like the white men whose hearts are ever filled with the fear of death, so when their time comes, they weep and wail and pray for a little more time so they may live their lives over again in a different manner.

NATIVE AMERICANA

OMAHA TRIBAL PROVERBS

"Stolen food never satisfies hunger."

"A poor man is a hard rider."

"All persons dislike a borrower."

"No one mourns the thriftless."

"The path of the lazy leads to disgrace."

"A man must make his own arrows."

"A handsome face does not make a good husband."

'Let neither cold, hunger, nor pain, nor the fear of them, neither the bristling teeth of danger nor the very jaws of death itself, prevent you from doing a good deed."
- Unknown Indian Chief

NATIVE AMERICANA

NATIVE AMERICAN WEAPONS

Offensive Weapons

Bow & Arrow

Bola

Tomahawk Axe

War Club

Spear

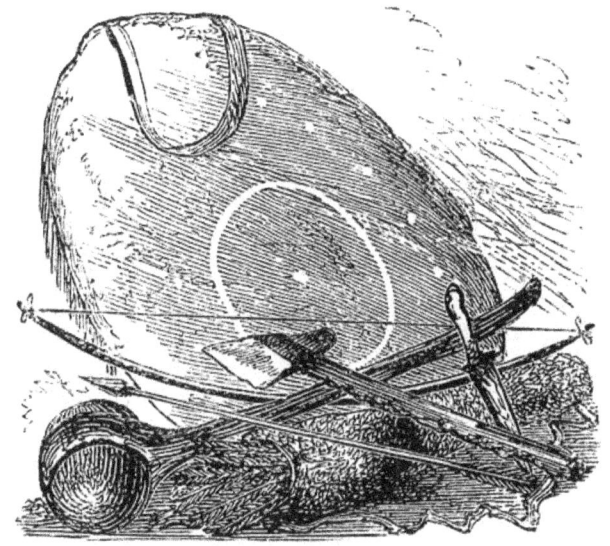

Defensive Weapons

Breastplate Armor

NATIVE AMERICANA

Shield

Helmet with visor

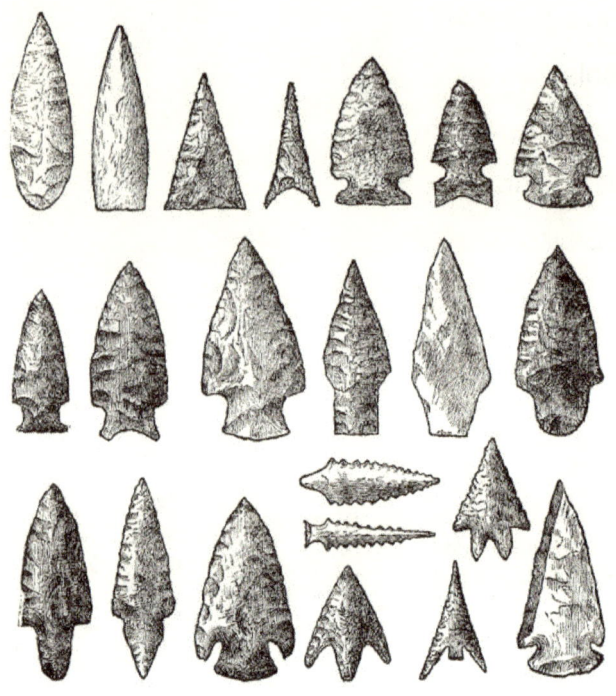

Arrowheads

Spear shooter

NATIVE AMERICANA

ALASKA REGION TRIBES

- Agdaagux Tribe of King Cove
- Akiachak Native Community
- Akiak Native Community
- Alatna Village
- Algaaciq Native Village (St. Mary's)
- Allakaket Village
- Alutiiq Tribe of Old Harbor
- Angoon Community Association
- Anvik Village
- Arctic Village
- Asa'carsarmiut Tribe
- Atqasuk Village (Atkasook)
- Beaver Village
- Birch Creek Tribe
- Central Council of the Tlingit & Haida Indian Tribes of Alaska
- Chalkyitsik Village
- Cheesh-Na Tribe
- Chevak Native Village
- Chickaloon Native Village
- Chignik Bay Tribal Council
- Chignik Lake Village
- Chilkat Indian Village (Klukwan)
- Chilkoot Indian Association (Haines)
- Chinik Eskimo Community (Golovin)
- Chuloonawick Native Village
- Circle Native Community
- Craig Tribal Association
- Curyung Tribal Council
- Douglas Indian Association
- Egegik Village

NATIVE AMERICANA

- Eklutna Native Village
- Emmonak Village
- Evansville Village (aka Bettles Field)
- Galena Village (aka Louden Village)
- Gulkana Village
- Healy Lake Village
- Holy Cross Village
- Hoonah Indian Association
- Hughes Village
- Huslia Village
- Hydaburg Cooperative Association
- Igiugig Village
- Inupiat Community of the Arctic Slope
- Iqurmuit Traditional Council
- Ivanof Bay Tribe
- Kaguyak Village
- Kaktovik Village (aka Barter Island)
- Kasigluk Traditional Elders Council
- Kenaitze Indian Tribe
- Ketchikan Indian Corporation
- King Island Native Community
- King Salmon Tribe
- Klawock Cooperative Association
- Knik Tribe
- Kokhanok Village
- Koyukuk Native Village
- Levelock Village
- Lime Village
- Manley Hot Springs Village
- Manokotak Village
- McGrath Native Village
- Mentasta Traditional Council
- Naknek Native Village

NATIVE AMERICANA

- Native Village of Afognak
- Native Village of Akhiok
- Native Village of Akutan
- Native Village of Aleknagik
- Native Village of Ambler
- Native Village of Atka
- Native Village of Barrow Inupiat Traditional Government
- Native Village of Belkofski
- Native Village of Brevig Mission
- Native Village of Buckland
- Native Village of Cantwell
- Native Village of Chenega (aka Chanega)
- Native Village of Chignik Lagoon
- Native Village of Chitina
- Native Village of Chuathbaluk (Russian Mission, Kuskokwim)
- Native Village of Council
- Native Village of Deering
- Native Village of Diomede (aka Inalik)
- Native Village of Eagle
- Native Village of Eek
- Native Village of Ekuk
- Native Village of Ekwok
- Native Village of Elim
- Native Village of Eyak (Cordova)
- Native Village of False Pass
- Native Village of Fort Yukon
- Native Village of Gakona
- Native Village of Gambell
- Native Village of Georgetown
- Native Village of Goodnews Bay
- Native Village of Hamilton

NATIVE AMERICANA

- Native Village of Hooper Bay
- Native Village of Kanatak
- Native Village of Karluk
- Native Village of Kiana
- Native Village of Kipnuk
- Native Village of Kivalina
- Native Village of Kluti-Kaah (aka Copper Center)
- Native Village of Kobuk
- Native Village of Kongiganak
- Native Village of Kotzebue
- Native Village of Koyuk
- Native Village of Kwigillingok
- Native Village of Kwinhagak (aka Quinhagak)
- Native Village of Larsen Bay
- Native Village of Marshall (aka Fortuna Ledge)
- Native Village of Mary's Igloo
- Native Village of Mekoryuk
- Native Village of Minto
- Native Village of Nanwalek (aka English Bay)
- Native Village of Napaimute
- Native Village of Napakiak
- Native Village of Napaskiak
- Native Village of Nelson Lagoon
- Native Village of Nightmute
- Native Village of Nikolski
- Native Village of Noatak
- Native Village of Nuiqsut (aka Nooiksut)
- Native Village of Nunam Iqua
- Native Village of Nunapitchuk
- Native Village of Ouzinkie
- Native Village of Paimiut
- Native Village of Perryville
- Native Village of Pilot Point

NATIVE AMERICANA

- Native Village of Pitka's Point
- Native Village of Point Hope
- Native Village of Point Lay
- Native Village of Port Graham
- Native Village of Port Heiden
- Native Village of Port Lions
- Native Village of Ruby
- Native Village of Saint Michael
- Native Village of Savoonga
- Native Village of Scammon Bay
- Native Village of Selawik
- Native Village of Shaktoolik
- Native Village of Shishmaref
- Native Village of Shungnak
- Native Village of Stevens
- Native Village of Tanacross
- Native Village of Tanana
- Native Village of Tatitlek
- Native Village of Tazlina
- Native Village of Teller
- Native Village of Tetlin
- Native Village of Tuntutuliak
- Native Village of Tununak
- Native Village of Tyonek
- Native Village of Unalakleet
- Native Village of Unga
- Native Village of Venetie Tribal Government
- Native Village of Wales
- Native Village of White Mountain
- Nenana Native Association
- New Koliganek Village Council
- New Stuyahok Village
- Newhalen Village

NATIVE AMERICANA

- Newtok Village
- Nikolai Village
- Ninilchik Village
- Nome Eskimo Community
- Nondalton Village
- Noorvik Native Community
- Northway Village
- Nulato Village
- Nunakauyarmiut Tribe
- Organized Village of Grayling (aka Holikachuk)
- Organized Village of Kake
- Organized Village of Kasaan
- Organized Village of Kwethluk
- Organized Village of Saxman
- Orutsararmiut Traditional Native Council
- Oscarville Traditional Village
- Pauloff Harbor Village
- Pedro Bay Village
- Petersburg Indian Association
- Pilot Station Traditional Village
- Platinum Traditional Village
- Portage Creek Village (aka Ohgsenakale)
- Qagan Tayagungin Tribe of Sand Point Village
- Qawalangin Tribe of Unalaska
- Rampart Village
- Saint George Island
- Saint Paul Island
- Seldovia Village Tribe
- Shageluk Native Village
- Sitka Tribe of Alaska
- Skagway Village
- South Naknek Village
- Stebbins Community Association

NATIVE AMERICANA

- Sun'aq Tribe of Kodiak
- Takotna Village
- Tangirnaq Native Village (aka Woody Island)
- Telida Village
- Traditional Village of Togiak
- Tuluksak Native Community
- Twin Hills Village
- Ugashik Village
- Umkumiut Native Village
- Village of Alakanuk
- Village of Anaktuvuk Pass
- Village of Aniak
- Village of Atmautluak
- Village of Bill Moore's Slough
- Village of Chefornak
- Village of Clarks Point
- Village of Crooked Creek
- Village of Dot Lake
- Village of Iliamna
- Village of Kalskag
- Village of Kaltag
- Village of Kotlik
- Village of Lower Kalskag
- Village of Ohogamiut
- Village of Red Devil
- Village of Salamatoff
- Village of Sleetmute
- Village of Solomon
- Village of Stony River
- Village of Venetie
- Village of Wainwright
- Wrangell Cooperative Association
- Yakutat Tlingit Tribe

NATIVE AMERICANA

- Yupiit of Andreafski

PACIFIC REGION TRIBES

- Agua Caliente Band of Cahuilla Indians of the Agua Caliente Indian Reservation, California
- Alturas Indian Rancheria, CA
- Augustine Band of Cahuilla Indians, California
- Bear River Band of the Rohnerville Rancheria, California
- Berry Creek Rancheria of Maidu Indians of California
- Big Lagoon Rancheria, California
- Big Pine Paiute Tribe of the Owens Valley
- Big Sandy Rancheria of Western Mono Indians of California
- Big Valley Band of Pomo Indians of the Big Valley Rancheria, California
- Bishop Paiute Tribe
- Blue Lake Rancheria, California
- Bridgeport Indian Colony
- Buena Vista Rancheria of Me-wuk Indians of California
- Cabazon Band of Mission Indians, California
- Cachil DeHe Band of Wintun Indians of the Colusa Indian Community of the Colusa Rancheria, California
- Cahto Tribe of the Laytonville Rancheria
- Cahuilla Band of Mission Indians of the Cahuilla Reservation, California
- California Valley Miwok Tribe, California
- Campo Band of Diegueno Mission Indians of the Campo Indian Reservation, California

NATIVE AMERICANA

- Capitan Grande Band of Diegueno Mission Indians of California (Barona Group of Capitan Grande Band of Mission Indians of the Barona Reservation, California)
- Capitan Grande Band of Diegueno Mission Indians of California: Viejas (Barona Long) Group of Capitan Grande Band of Mission Indians of the Viejas Reservation, California
- Cedarville Rancheria, California
- Cher-Ae Heights Indian Community of the Trinidad Rancheria, California
- Chicken Ranch Rancheria of Me-wuk Indians of California
- Cloverdale Rancheria of Pomo Indians of California
- Cold Springs Rancheria of Mono Indians of California
- Coyote Valley Band of Pomo Indians of California
- Death Valley Timbi-sha Shoshone Tribe
- Dry Creek Rancheria Band of Pomo Indians, California
- Elem Indian Colony of Pomo Indians of the Sulphur Bank Rancheria, California
- Elk Valley Rancheria, California
- Enterprise Rancheria of Maidu Indians of California
- Ewiiaapaayp Band of Kumeyaay Indians, California
- Federated Indians of Graton Rancheria, California
- Fort Bidwell Indian Community of the Fort Bidwell Reservation of California

NATIVE AMERICANA

- Fort Independence Indian Community of Paiute Indians of the Fort Independence Reservation, California
- Greenville Rancheria
- Grindstone Indian Rancheria of Wintun-Wailaki Indians of California
- Guidiville Rancheria of California
- Habematolel Pomo of Upper Lake, California
- Hoopa Valley Tribe, California
- Hopland Band of Pomo Indians, California
- Iipay Nation of Santa Ysabel, California
- Inaja Band of Diegueno Mission Indians of the Inaja and Cosmit Reservation, California
- Ione Band of Miwok Indians of California
- Jackson Band of Miwuk Indians
- Jamul Indian Village of California
- Karuk Tribe
- Kashia Band of Pomo Indians of the Stewarts Point Rancheria, California
- Kletsel Dehe Band of Wintun Indians
- Koi Nation of Northern California
- La Jolla Band of Luiseno Indians, California
- La Posta Band of Diegueno Mission Indians of the La Posta Indian Reservation, California
- Lone Pine Paiute-Shoshone Tribe
- Los Coyotes Band of Cahuilla & Cupeno Indians, California
- Lytton Rancheria of California
- Manchester Band of Pomo Indians of the Manchester Rancheria, California
- Manzanita Band of Diegueno Mission Indians of the Manzanita Reservation, Califonria

NATIVE AMERICANA

- Mechoopda Indian Tribe of Chico Rancheria, California
- Mesa Grande Band of Diegueno Mission Indians of the Mesa Grande Reservation, California
- Middletown Rancheria of Pomo Indians of California
- Mooretown Rancheria of Maidu Indians of California
- Morongo Band of Mission Indians, California
- Northfork Rancheria of Mono Indians of California
- Pala Band of Mission Indians
- Paskenta Band of Nomlaki Indians of California
- Pauma Band of Luiseno Mission Indians of the Pauma & Yuima Reservation, California
- Pechanga Band of Luiseno Mission Indians of the Pechanga Reservation, California
- Picayune Rancheria of Chukchansi Indians of California
- Pinoleville Pomo Nation, California
- Pit River Tribe, California
- Potter Valley Tribe, California
- Quartz Valley Indian Community of the Quartz Valley Reservation of California
- Ramona Band of Cahuilla, California
- Redding Rancheria, California
- Redwood Valley or Little River Band of Pomo Indians of the Redwood Valley Rancheria California
- Resighini Rancheria, California
- Rincon Band of Luiseno Mission Indians of the Rincon Reservation, California
- Robinson Rancheria Band of Pomo Indians, CA

NATIVE AMERICANA

- Round Valley Indian Tribes, Round Valley Reservation, California
- San Manuel Band of Mission Indians, California
- San Pasqual Band of Diegueno Mission Indians of California
- Santa Rosa Band of Cahuilla Indians, California
- Santa Rosa Indian Community of the Santa Rosa Rancheria, California
- Santa Ynez Band of Chumash Mission Indians of the Santa Ynez Reservation, California
- Scotts Valley Band of Pomo Indians of California
- Sherwood Valley Rancheria of Pomo Indians of California
- Shingle Springs Band of Miwok Indians, Shingle Springs Rancheria (Verona Tract), California
- Soboba Band of Luiseno Indians, California
- Susanville Indian Rancheria, California
- Sycuan Band of the Kumeyaay Nation
- Table Mountain Rancheria of California
- Tejon Indian Tribe
- Tolowa Dee-Ni' Nation
- Torres Martinez Desert Cahuilla Indians, California
- Tule River Indian Tribe of the Tule River Reservation, California
- Tuolumne Band of Me-Wuk Indians of the Tuolumne Rancheria of California
- Twenty-Nine Palms Band of Mission Indians of California
- United Auburn Indian Community of the Auburn Rancheria of California
- Utu Utu Gwaitu Paiute Tribe of the Benton Paiute Reservation, California

NATIVE AMERICANA

- Wilton Rancheria
- Wiyot Tribe, California
- Yocha Dehe Wintun Nation, California
- Yurok Tribe of the Yurok Reservation, California

NORTHWEST REGION

- Burns Paiute Tribe
- Coeur D'Alene Tribe
- Confederated Salish & Kootenai Tribes of the Flathead Reservation
- Confederated Tribes and Bands of the Yakama Nation
- Confederated Tribes of Coos, Lower Umpqua and Siuslaw Indians
- Confederated Tribes of Siletz Indians of Oregon
- Confederated Tribes of the Chehalis Reservation
- Confederated Tribes of the Colville Reservation
- Confederated Tribes of the Grand Ronde Community of Oregon
- Confederated Tribes of the Umatilla Indian Reservation
- Confederated Tribes of the Warm Springs Reservation of Oregon
- Coquille Indian Tribe
- Cow Creek Band of Umpqua Tribe of Indians
- Cowlitz Indian Tribe
- Hoh Indian Tribe
- Jamestown S'Klallam Tribe
- Kalispel Indian Community of the Kalispel Reservation
- Klamath Tribes

NATIVE AMERICANA

- Kootenai Tribe of Idaho
- Lower Elwha Tribal Community
- Lummi Tribe of the Lummi Reservation
- Makah Indian Tribe of the Makah Indian Reservation
- Muckleshoot Indian Tribe
- Nez Perce Tribe
- Nisqually Indian Tribe
- Nooksack Indian Tribe
- Northwestern Band of Shoshone Nation
- Port Gamble S'Klallam Tribe
- Puyallup Tribe of the Puyallup Reservation
- Quileute Tribe of the Quileute Reservation
- Quinault Indian Nation
- Samish Indian Nation
- Sauk-Suiattle Indian Tribe
- Shoalwater Bay Indian Tribe
- Shoshone-Bannock Tribes of the Fort Hall Reservation
- Skokomish Indian Tribe
- Snoqualmie Indian Tribe
- Spokane Tribe of the Spokane Reservation
- Squaxin Island Tribe of the Squaxin Island Reservation
- Stillaguamish Tribe of Indians of Washington
- Suquamish Indian Tribe of the Port Madison Reservation
- Swinomish Indian Tribal Community
- Tulalip Tribes of Washington
- Upper Skagit Indian Tribe
- Metlakatla Indian Community, Annette Island Reserve

NATIVE AMERICANA

Pocahontas

NATIVE AMERICANA

WESTERN REGION TRIBES
- Colorado River Agency
- Eastern Nevada Agency
- Fort Apache Agency
- Fort Yuma Agency
- Hopi Agency
- Papago Agency
- Pima Agency
- Salt River Agency
- San Carlos Agency
- Southern Paiute Agency
- Truxton Canon Agency
- Uintah & Ouray Agency
- Western Nevada Agency
- Western Regional Office
- Ak-Chin Indian Community of the Maricopa (Ak Chin) Indian Reservation, Arizona
- Chemehuevi Indian Tribe of the Chemehuevi Reservation, California
- Cocopah Tribe of Arizona
- Colorado River Indian Tribes of the Colorado Indian Reservation, Arizona and California
- Confederated Tribes of the Goshute Reservation, Nevada and Utah
- Duckwater Shoshone Tribe of the Duckwater Reservation, Nevada
- Ely Shoshone Tribe of Nevada
- Fort McDermitt Paiute and Shoshone Tribes of the Fort McDermitt Indian Reservation, Nevada and Oregon
- Fort McDowell Yavapai Nation, Arizona
- Fort Mojave Indian Tribe of Arizona, California & Nevada

NATIVE AMERICANA

- Gila River Indian Community of the Gila River Indian Reservation, Arizona
- Havasupai Tribe of the Havasupai Reservation, Arizona
- Hopi Tribe of Arizona
- Hualapai Indian Tribe of the Hualapai Indian Reservation, Arizona
- Kaibab Band of Paiute Indians of the Kaibab Indian Reservation, Arizona
- Las Vegas Tribe of Paiute Indians of the Las Vegas Indian Colony, Nevada
- Lovelock Paiute Tribe of the Lovelock Indian Colony, Nevada
- Moapa Band of Paiute Indians of the Moapa River Indian Reservation, Nevada
- Paiute Indian Tribe of Utah (Cedar Band of Paiutes, Kanosh Band of Paiutes, Koosharem Band of Paiutes, Indian Peaks Band of Paiutes, and Shivwits Band of Paiutes)
- Paiute-Shoshone Tribe of the Fallon Reservation and Colony, Nevada
- Pascua Yaqui Tribe of Arizona
- Pyramid Lake Paiute Tribe of the Pyramid Lake Reservation, Nevada
- Quechan Tribe of the Fort Yuma Indian Reservation, California & Arizona
- Reno-Sparks Indian Colony, Nevada
- Salt River Pima-Maricopa Indian Community of the Salt River Reservation, Arizona
- San Carlos Apache Tribe of the San Carlos Reservation, Arizona
- San Juan Southern Paiute Tribe of Arizona
- Shoshone-Paiute Tribes of the Duck Valley Reservation, Nevada

NATIVE AMERICANA

- Skull Valley Band of Goshute Indians of Utah
- Summit Lake Paiute Tribe of Nevada
- Te-Moak Tribe of Western Shoshone Indians of Nevada (Four constituent bands: Battle Mountain Band; Elko Band; South Fork Band and Wells Band)
- Tohono O'odham Nation of Arizona
- Tonto Apache Tribe of Arizona
- Ute Indian Tribe of the Uintah & Ouray Reservation, Utah
- Walker River Paiute Tribe of the Walker River Reservation, Nevada
- Washoe Tribe of Nevada & California (Carson Colony, Dresslerville Colony, Woodfords Community, Stewart Community, & Washoe Ranches)
- White Mountain Apache Tribe of the Fort Apache Reservation, Arizona
- Winnemucca Indian Colony of Nevada
- Yavapai-Apache Nation of the Camp Verde Indian Reservation, Arizona
- Yavapai-Prescott Indian Tribe
- Yerington Paiute Tribe of the Yerington Colony & Campbell Ranch, Nevada

SOUTHWESTERN REGION TRIBES
- Jicarilla Apache Nation, New Mexico
- Kewa Pueblo
- Mescalero Apache Tribe
- Ohkay Owingeh
- Pueblo of Acoma
- Pueblo of Cochiti
- Pueblo of Isleta

NATIVE AMERICANA

- Pueblo of Jemez
- Pueblo of Laguna
- Pueblo of Nambe
- Pueblo of Picuris
- Pueblo of Pojoaque
- Pueblo of San Felipe
- Pueblo of San Ildefonso
- Pueblo of Sandia
- Pueblo of Santa Ana
- Pueblo of Santa Clara
- Pueblo of Taos
- Pueblo of Tesuque
- Pueblo of Zia
- Ramah Navajo Chapter
- Southern Ute Indian Tribe
- Ute Mountain Ute Tribe
- Ysleta del Sur Pueblo
- Zuni Tribe of the Zuni Reservation

SOUTHERN PLAINS REGION
- Absentee-Shawnee Tribe of Indians of Oklahoma
- Alabama-Coushatta Tribes of Texas
- Apache Tribe of Oklahoma
- Caddo Nation of Oklahoma
- Cheyenne and Arapaho Tribes, Oklahoma
- Citizen Potawatomi Nation (Oklahoma)
- Comanche Nation, Oklahoma
- Delaware Nation, Oklahoma
- Fort Sill Apache Tribe of Oklahoma
- Iowa Tribe of Kansas & Nebraska
- Iowa Tribe of Oklahoma
- Kaw Nation, Oklahoma

NATIVE AMERICANA

- Kickapoo Traditional Tribe of Texas
- Kickapoo Tribe of Indians of the Kickapoo Reservation in Kansas
- Kickapoo Tribe of Oklahoma
- Kiowa Indian Tribe of Oklahoma
- Otoe-Missouria Tribe of Indians, Oklahoma
- Pawnee Nation of Oklahoma
- Ponca Tribe of Indians of Oklahoma
- Prairie Band of Potawatomi Nation
- Sac and Fox Nation of Missouri in Kansas and Nebraska
- Sac and Fox Nation, Oklahoma
- Tonkawa Tribe of Indians of Oklahoma
- Wichita and Affiliated Tribes

EASTERN OKLAHOMA REGION

- Alabama-Quassarte Tribal Town
- Cherokee Nation
- Delaware Tribe of Indians
- Eastern Shawnee Tribe of Oklahoma
- Kialegee Tribal Town
- Miami Tribe of Oklahoma
- Ottawa Tribe of Oklahoma
- Peoria Tribe of Indians of Oklahoma
- Seneca-Cayuga Nation
- Shawnee Tribe
- The Chickasaw Nation
- The Choctaw Nation of Oklahoma
- The Modoc Tribe of Oklahoma
- The Muscogee (Creek) Nation
- The Osage Nation
- The Quapaw Tribe of Indians

NATIVE AMERICANA

- The Seminole Nation of Oklahoma
- Thlopthlocco Tribal Town
- United Keetoowah Band of Cherokee Indians in Oklahoma
- Wyandotte Nation

EASTERN REGION
- Aroostook Band of Micmacs
- Catawba Indian Nation
- Cayuga Nation
- Chitimacha Tribe of Louisiana
- Coushatta Tribe of Louisiana
- Eastern Band of Cherokee Indians
- Houlton Band of Maliseet Indians
- Jena Band of Choctaw Indians
- Mashantucket Pequot Indian Tribe
- Mashpee Wampanoag Tribe
- Miccosukee Tribe of Indians
- Mississippi Band of Choctaw Indians
- Mohegan Tribe of Indians of Connecticut
- Narragansett Indian Tribe
- Oneida Nation of New York
- Onondaga Nation
- Pamunkey Indian Tribe
- Passamaquoddy Tribe - Indian Township
- Passamaquoddy Tribe - Pleasant Point
- Penobscot Nation
- Poarch Band of Creeks
- Saint Regis Mohawk Tribe
- Seminole Tribe of Florida
- Seneca Nation of Indians
- Shinnecock Indian Nation
- Tonawanda Band of Seneca

NATIVE AMERICANA

- Tunica-Biloxi Indian Tribe
- Tuscarora Nation
- Wampanoag Tribe of Gay Head (Aquinnah)

MIDWEST REGION
- Bad River Band of Lake Superior Tribe of Chippewa Indians
- Bay Mills Indian Community, Michigan
- Forest County Potawatomi Community, Wisconsin
- Grand Traverse Band of Ottawa & Chippewa Indians, Michigan
- Hannahville Indian Community, Michigan
- Ho-Chunk Nation of Wisconsin
- Keweenaw Bay Indian Community, Michigan
- Lac Courte Oreilles Band of Lake Superior Chippewa Indians of Wisconsin
- Lac du Flambeau Band of Lake Superior Chippewa Indians of Wisconsin
- Lac Vieux Desert Band of Lake Superior Chippewa Indians of MI
- Little River Band of Ottawa Indians, Michigan
- Little Traverse Bay Bands of Odawa Indians, Michigan
- Lower Sioux Indian Community in the State of Minnesota
- Match-e-be-nash-she-wish Band of Pottawatomi Indians of Michigan
- Menominee Indian Tribe of Wisconsin
- Minnesota Chippewa Tribe
- Minnesota Chippewa Tribe - Bois Forte Band (Nett Lake)
- Minnesota Chippewa Tribe - Fond du Lac Band

NATIVE AMERICANA

- Minnesota Chippewa Tribe - Grand Portage Band
- Minnesota Chippewa Tribe - Leech Lake Band
- Minnesota Chippewa Tribe - Mille Lacs Band
- Minnesota Chippewa Tribe - White Earth Band
- Nottawaseppi Huron Band of the Potawatomi, MI
- Oneida Nation
- Pokagon Band of Potawatomi Indians, Michigan & Indiana
- Prairie Island Indian Community in the State of MN
- Red Cliff Band of Lake Superior Chippewa Indians of Wisconsin
- Red Lake Band of Chippewa Indians, Minnesota
- Sac & Fox Tribe of the Mississippi in Iowa
- Saginaw Chippewa Indian Tribe of Michigan
- Sault Ste. Marie Tribe of Chippewa Indians, Michigan
- Shakopee Mdewakanton Sioux Community of Minnesota
- Sokaogon Chippewa Community, Wisconsin
- St. Croix Chippewa Indians of Wisconsin
- Stockbridge Munsee Community, Wisconsin
- Upper Sioux Community, Minnesota

GREAT PLAINS REGION
- Cheyenne River Sioux Tribe of the Cheyenne River Reservation, SD
- Crow Creek Sioux Tribe of the Crow Creek Reservation, SD
- Flandreau Santee Sioux Tribe of South Dakota

NATIVE AMERICANA

- Lower Brule Sioux Tribe of the Lower Brule Reservation, SD
- Oglala Sioux Tribe
- Omaha Tribe of Nebraska
- Ponca Tribe of Nebraska
- Rosebud Sioux Tribe of the Rosebud Indian Reservation, SD
- Santee Sioux Nation, Nebraska
- Sisseton-Wahpeton Oyate of the Lake Traverse Reservation, SD
- Spirit Lake Tribe, North Dakota
- Standing Rock Sioux Tribe of North & South Dakota
- Three Affiliated Tribes of the Fort Berthold Reservation, ND
- Turtle Mountain Band of Chippewa Indians of North Dakota
- Winnebago Tribe of Nebraska
- Yankton Sioux Tribe of South Dakota

ROCKY MOUNTAIN REGION

- Assiniboine & Sioux Tribes of the Fort Peck Indian Reservation, MT
- Blackfeet Tribe of the Blackfeet Indian Reservation of MT
- Chippewa Cree Indians of the Rocky Boy's Reservation, MT
- Crow Tribe of Montana
- Eastern Shoshone Tribe of the Wind River Reservation, Wyoming
- Fort Belknap Indian Community

NATIVE AMERICANA

- Northern Arapaho Tribe of the Wind River Reservation, Wyoming
- Northern Cheyenne Tribe

NAVAJO REGION

- Navajo Nation, Arizona, New Mexico & Utah

NATIVE AMERICANA

THE LAST WORD

I hope you have learned much from reading this book and I am hopeful that the Native American way of life can inspire you in your own life. The Native American people have faced much hardship and difficulty. I hope that the various tribes can work together to create a stronger unity that will create long lasting benefits for their people. The Native American people are an inspiration to me and their culture is both admirable as well as familiar. Thank you for reading this book.

Sincerely,
Kambiz Mostofizadeh

NATIVE AMERICANA

NOTES

NATIVE AMERICANA

NOTES

NATIVE AMERICANA

NOTES

NATIVE AMERICANA

NOTES

NATIVE AMERICANA

NOTES

NATIVE AMERICANA

NOTES

NATIVE AMERICANA

NOTES

NATIVE AMERICANA

NOTES

NATIVE AMERICANA

ACKNOWLEDGMENTS

Thank you to:

Shervin Khoramianpour

500 Tribes

California State University Dominguez Hills

My Family and Friends

Southwest Museum

Morongo Tribe

Professor Annie Whetmore PHD

www.ingramcontent.com/pod-product-compliance
Lightning Source LLC
LaVergne TN
LVHW011205080426
835508LV00007B/604